Animal Neighbours
Toad

Stephen Savage

H O D D E R
Wayland
An imprint of Hodder Children's Books

Animal Neighbours

Titles in this series:

Badger • Bat • Blackbird • Deer • Duck • Fox
Hare • Hedgehog • Mole • Mouse • Otter • Owl
Rat • Snake • Swallow • Toad

**For more information on this series and other Hodder Wayland titles,
go to www.hodderwayland.co.uk**

Conceived and produced for Hodder Wayland by

Nutshell
MEDIA

Intergen House, 65–67 Western Road, Hove BN3 2JQ, UK
www.nutshellmedialtd.co.uk

Commissioning Editor: Vicky Brooker
Editor: Polly Goodman
Designer: Mayer Media Ltd
Illustrator: Jackie Harland

Published in Great Britain in 2005 by Hodder Wayland, an imprint of Hodder Children's Books.

British Library Cataloguing in Publication Data
Savage, Stephen, 1965–
Toad. – (Animal neighbours)
1. Toads – Juvenile literature
I. Title
597.8'7

ISBN 0 7502 4661 8

Cover: A common toad keeps a watchful lookout for passing insects.
Title page: A toad catches a worm with its sticky tongue.

Picture acknowledgements
FLPA 10 (Foto Natura Stock), 13 (Chris Mattison), 14 (John Tinning), 29 top right (Roger Tidman); OSF *Cover* (Manfred Pfefferie), 6 (Mike Linley), 7 (Michael Fogden), 8 (Ian West), 9 (OSF), 12, 20, 21, 25 (Paulo de Oliveira), 26 (Michael Leach), 27 (Ian West), 28 top (OSF); naturepl.com 11 top, middle & bottom (Fabio Liverani), 15 (George McCarthy), 17 (Jose B. Ruiz), 28 right & bottom (Fabio Liverani); NHPA *Title page* (Stephen Dalton), 16 (Ernie Janes), 19 (Stephen Dalton), 22 (Manfred Danegger), 23 (Daniel Heuchlin), 24 (Yves Lanceau), 28 left (Manfred Danegger).

Printed and bound in China.

Hodder Children's Books
A division of Hodder Headline Limited
338 Euston Road, London NW1 3BH

Contents

Meet the Toad   4

The Toad Family   6

Birth and Growing Up   8

Habitat   12

Food   18

Finding a Mate   22

Threats   24

Toad Life Cycle   28

Toad Clues   29

Glossary   30

Finding Out More   31

Index   32

Meet the Toad

Toads are plump, tailless amphibians. Being amphibian means they spend part of their lives in water and part on land. There are over 300 species of toads. They live mainly in damp habitats, including ponds, rivers and ditches.

This book is about the common European toad, the largest toad in Europe.

▲ **The red part of this map shows where the common European toad lives in the world today.**

Skin

The skin is dry and lumpy. Its colour camouflages the toad amongst its surroundings. Poison is released through the skin as a defence against predators.

Hind feet

The hind feet have five partly webbed toes that help the toad when swimming. Small claws on the ends of the toes help dig holes for resting or hibernation.

TOAD FACTS

The common toad's scientific name is *Bufo bufo*, which comes from the Latin word *bufo* meaning 'toad'.

Toads lay eggs that hatch into tadpoles. Once they have grown four legs the tadpoles are called toadlets.

Females are larger than the males. Male toads grow up to 7 cm long and weigh up to 50 g. Females grow up to 13 cm and weigh up to 120 g.

▲ **A common toad.**

Ears

Toads have no external ears. An eardrum just beneath the skin is used to hear courtship calls and may detect predators.

Eyes

Large eyes set high up on the head provide the toad with its most important sense. The eyes never close, but they are protected by a special 'third eyelid'. This is a clear membrane that can be drawn across the eyes to keep them free of debris and help the toad to see under water.

Nostrils

Two nostrils on the end of the snout let the toad breathe with only its snout above water. Toads may use smell to find breeding ponds.

Mouth

The mouth can open wide enough to eat large prey, such as newts and lizards. The long, sticky tongue inside is up to 10 cm long. It is flicked out to catch prey.

Poison glands

Two large glands behind the eyes produce a foul-tasting and irritating substance, which is used in defence against predators.

Front feet

The front feet have four toes that are not webbed. Male toads have dark-coloured nuptial pads (swellings) on three of their front toes, which grow bigger in the breeding season and help them grip on to a female toad during mating.

▲ **This shows the size of the common toad compared to an adult human hand.**

The Toad Family

Toads are closely related to frogs, newts and salamanders. Frogs and toads are very similar, but newts and salamanders are different. They have long, thin bodies and a tail.

Frogs and toads are the largest group of amphibians, with over 3,900 different species. Toads are actually types of frog, but they have certain physical characteristics that can be used to tell them apart (see box on page 7).

Most toads abandon their eggs and leave their tadpole young to fend for themselves. However a few species, such as the midwife toad from Western and Central Europe, take great care of their eggs. While the eggs are developing, the male midwife toad carries them on his back and only deposits them in a pond when they are ready to hatch.

▼ During dry weather, a male midwife toad will enter the water at night to prevent the eggs drying out on his back.

Not all toads live in damp places. The Couch's spadefoot toad lives in desert regions of the USA. It lies asleep in underground burrows until the rainy season, when it wakes up and lays its eggs in puddles.

Many toads are brown-coloured to hide them from predators but a few species, such as the fire-bellied toad from Asia, are brightly coloured. If disturbed, this toad flips on its back to show its bright red belly. It warns predators that the toad is poisonous.

WHAT'S THE DIFFERENCE?

Toads differ from frogs in the following ways:

- Toads have lumpy skin; frogs have smooth skin.

- Toads have broad bodies and short hind legs, which are well-suited to walking and crawling; frogs have longer legs more suited to leaping.

- Toads do not have any teeth; frogs have tiny teeth.

▼ When threatened, the fire-bellied toad shows its red underside to frighten away predators.

Birth and Growing Up

It is spring, and a female toad looks for an area of weed on a pond to lay her eggs. With a male clinging to her back, she lays between 600 and 4,000 eggs. As the eggs are laid they are fertilized by the male.

It may take between 10 and 28 hours to lay all the eggs, which are protected within a string of jelly. As the eggs are laid they coil around the pondweed, which anchors them in place.

▼ Masses of eggs are laid by the adults because many of the tadpoles will be eaten by predators.

EGGS

Toad eggs are round and black, inside a string of jelly. The eggs are arranged in two rows. This differs from frogs' eggs, which are laid in a clump.

The eggs are usually laid in March, but they may be laid as early as February if the weather is warm, or as late as the end of April if it is cold.

A group of eggs in jelly is called spawn.

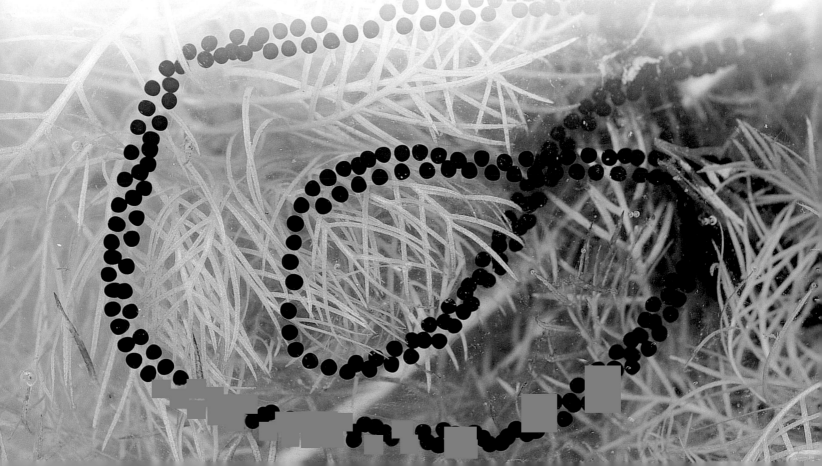

▲ These tiny,
five-day-old toad
embryos are growing
inside the protective
jelly of the spawn.

Once they have been laid, the female leaves the eggs
to develop by themselves. After ten days, the eggs
hatch into tiny tadpoles. The tadpoles are not very
good swimmers and attach themselves to the outside
of the jelly string or to nearby plants for the next two
or three days. They hold on using a special sticky
organ on their undersides. The tadpoles are fed by the
remains of the egg yolk still inside their stomach.

▲ These two-week-old toad tadpoles breathe using external gills.

Early days

The tadpoles leave the jelly string after a few days and swim together in a shoal. They swim using their tail in a side-to-side, wriggling movement.

At this stage, the tadpoles are just an oval body and tail, about 4–6 millimetres long. Unlike adult toads, which have lungs, tadpoles have feathery gills for breathing under water. They have poor eyesight and can see little more than light and dark. To eat, tadpoles scrape algae off rocks and pond plants using rough parts in their mouths.

DEVELOPMENT

The development of a tadpole is greatly affected by the weather and water temperatures. The average time it takes for a tadpole to develop into a toad is 13 weeks. However, in warm weather it may do so within 9 weeks and in colder weather it may take as long as 16 weeks. Tadpoles develop more slowly during colder weather, and in colder countries.

▲ At 7–9 weeks, the tadpole grows back legs.

▲ At 11–12 weeks, the tadpole grows front legs.

▼ When the toadlets leave the water, some still have their tails.

By the time it is 4 weeks old, the tadpole will have grown to about 10 millimetres long. The external gills are absorbed and replaced by gills inside the body. Between 7–9 weeks of age the tadpole grows back legs. The front legs develop at around 11–12 weeks, when the body shape begins to resemble an adult. Over the next week or two, the tail is absorbed into the body and the tiny toadlet leaves the pond with many of the characteristics of its parents.

Before they leave the water, dragonfly larvae, predatory beetles and other predators kill and eat the tadpoles. However, fewer toad tadpoles are eaten by predators than frog tadpoles because they taste unpleasant.

Habitat

We usually think of toads as pond creatures, but the common toad spends most of its adult life on land. It only returns to water to breed, or during very dry weather. Common toads live in most habitats, from lakes and large ponds to slow-moving rivers and ditches. They also live in woodlands, forests, fields and other grasslands.

▼ Toads have drier skin than frogs, so they can live further away from water. This one is on the edge of a woodland.

▲ **This toad is hiding amongst some damp fungi.**

Toads like damp places to keep their skin moist and plenty of vegetation to hide beneath. On farmland, they live under hedgerows and use the irrigation ditches for breeding in the spring.

Toads are mainly nocturnal, which means they are most active at night. In the daytime, they rest in places hidden from predators. These might be shallow burrows, beneath large stones or logs, in long vegetation or beneath leaf litter. Toads gather together in large numbers during the breeding season, but for the rest of the year they live alone.

Urban habitats

Toads have adapted well to a variety of urban habitats. They are often found in churchyards, wasteland, or other places with lots of overgrown vegetation. Such habitats have plenty of places to hide from predators and are usually undisturbed by people. They are also good sources of food, such as worms, slugs and insects.

Toads may also be found in parks and gardens, either with or without ponds, as long as there are bushes or other vegetation for cover. They are agile animals that can climb garden walls and fences. In gardens, they may be found resting in greenhouses, sheds or cellars, and beneath compost heaps.

▼ Toads visit ponds in gardens, parks and allotments in the spring to breed.

TOAD TUNNELS

In places where large numbers of toads travel across roads to reach breeding ponds, road signs are sometimes put up to warn motorists to slow down, so they can see and try to avoid the toads. On busy main roads, toad tunnels are sometimes built so that the toads can travel safely underneath the road.

◀ These toads have just crossed safely beneath a busy road using a special toad tunnel.

Toads often breed in garden ponds. They help gardeners by eating slugs, snails and other garden pests. People can attract toads and frogs to their ponds by adding ramps at the edges, which make it easier for them to get in and out. Growing plants around the edge of a pond provides cover for the young when they leave.

Hibernation

In parts of Britain and Europe, where it gets very cold in the winter, there is not enough food for toads to eat and their bodies become too cold to remain active. To survive these conditions, toads hibernate for the winter months.

Common toads usually start to hibernate from the middle of October. They look for somewhere sheltered, such as the roots of a large tree, a rock or an empty animal burrow, and dig a hole. They use their hind legs to dig the hole, which is about 45 centimetres deep.

▲ This toad is leaving the hollow tree where it spent the winter in hibernation.

TOAD IN THE HOLE

Even though people don't eat toads, there is an English dish called 'Toad in the Hole'. It was named after the toad's habit of hibernating underground. This dish, which originated in Yorkshire, in northern England, is made from sausages cooked in batter.

In gardens, toads hibernate in greenhouses, sheds or rockeries, which are warmer than outside. Compost heaps are favourite hibernation sites because they are damp and the decomposing vegetation gives off heat.

While it is hibernating, the toad's heart rate and breathing slow right down. To survive without eating, the toad lives off its reserves of body fat, which have been built up throughout the summer. Around the middle of March, the toad wakes up and begins its journey back to its breeding pond. For some toads this may be as far as 3 kilometres. Since toads travel at a speed of 50–150 metres an hour, this journey can take up to five days. If the weather turns cold again during the journey, the toad will burrow underground and sleep until it gets warm enough to continue.

▼ **A toad starts the long walk to the pond where it hatched.**

Food

Tadpoles and adult toads eat very different types of food. Tadpoles feed mainly on plants, using their rasping mouthparts to scrape algae from pondweed. Tadpoles are omnivores because although they feed mainly on plants, they will also swallow microscopic pond creatures. If a pond becomes overcrowded, toad tadpoles may even feed on each other.

▼ Toads are in the middle of their food chain. Crows and some other predators are thought to eat the flesh but leave the skin.

Toad food chain

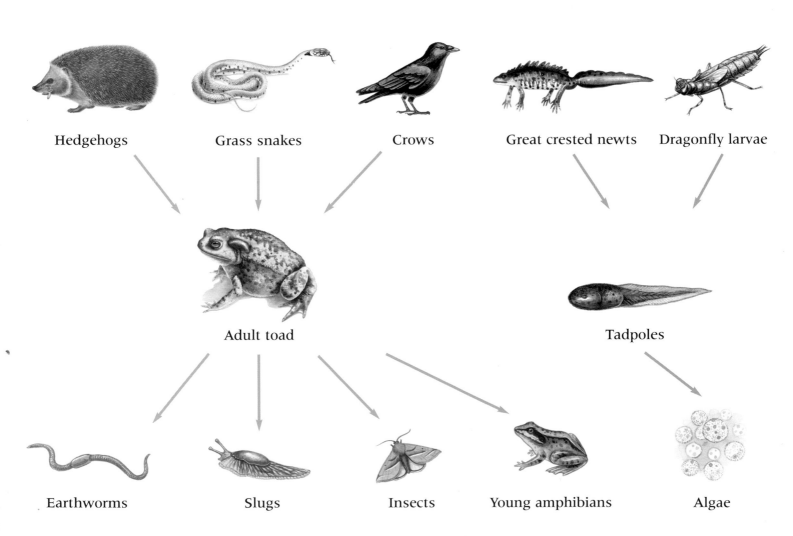

Hedgehogs

Grass snakes

Crows

Great crested newts

Dragonfly larvae

Adult toad

Tadpoles

Earthworms

Slugs

Insects

Young amphibians

Algae

The illustrations are not to scale.

▼ **Earthworms provide toads with both food and water, since their bodies are made up of 85 per cent water.**

Adult toads are carnivores. They catch their prey from the ground and from the air. Toads eat a wide variety of prey, including earthworms, slugs, spiders, beetles, flies, woodlice and caterpillars. They also eat larger animals such as young frogs, lizards and newts. Adult toads feed a great deal during the spring and summer to replace the body reserves used up during hibernation and mating.

Hunting

▲ The tongue flicks out in the blink of an eye to catch a moth in flight.

Toads hunt mainly at night, when the air is cool and damp. This is also the time when their prey is most active and most of their predators are asleep. Toads catch their prey with their long tongue, which has a sticky pad on the end.

Toads have two main ways of finding prey. The first is simply to sit and wait for something to pass within reach. When a victim comes close, the toad flicks out its tongue so the sticky pad on the end attaches to its victim, then rapidly pulls the tongue back into its mouth.

AUTOMATIC REFLEX

Toads have an automatic feeding reflex. Their large eyes are very sensitive to movement and once they detect moving prey, the tongue automatically flicks out at its target. This feeding reflex will only be triggered by things that are moving slowly and are small enough to eat. However, the toad often misses on the first attempt.

Toads also hunt for food using the two large eyes on the top of their head. When a toad spots something, it quietly creeps up close to its victim before lunging at the prey with its mouth open as its sticky tongue flicks out.

Toads do not have teeth to chew their food or saliva to help them swallow. Instead, they crush their prey against the roof of their mouth before swallowing it whole. To help them swallow, toads pull their eyeballs back into their head, which helps push large food items down their throat and into their stomach.

▼ A toad pulls its eyeballs back into its head to help force a large centipede down its throat.

Finding a Mate

Female toads are old enough to breed when they are 3 or 4 years old, but male toads mature older, when they are 4 or 5. As soon as they wake up from hibernation, mature toads make their way to a breeding pond. This is usually the same pond every year and is the pond where they originally hatched. Sometimes male toads hitch a ride to the breeding pond by clinging to a female's back.

There are usually more male toads than females, so the males compete for the females by croaking. The males with the deepest croaks attract the females. Once a female accepts a male, he climbs on her back and holds on using special nuptial pads on his thumbs. Other males may jostle him and try to take his place. If a toad with a deeper croak approaches, the first male will give up the female.

▼ A male toad holds on to the body of a larger female as he prepares to mate. This position is called amplexus.

CROAKING COURTSHIP

Only male toads can croak. They croak to attract females. A male will also croak if another male mistakes him for a female and climbs on his back. This is called a release call. Compared with other toads and frogs, the common toad's croak is quiet. This is because it lacks the large vocal sac that many frogs have, which makes their calls louder.

Once on her back, a male holds on to a female for a few days until she has laid all her eggs, fertilizing them as they are released. Once the female has laid her eggs, she will leave the pond and not return until the following year.

▼ Here, several male toads are struggling to mate with one female.

Threats

Common toads can live for up to 50 years, although most live for 8–10 years. Many predators, including cats, herons and seagulls, will kill toads but not eat them. This is because they produce a poison through their skin which gives them a sour taste. A few animals, such as grass snakes, hedgehogs and crows, seem able to eat toads despite their foul-tasting skin.

Dogs and other animals with a good sense of smell are often put off by the scent of a toad. If they do pick one up in their mouth, they usually drop it again quickly.

▲ A cat toys with a toad, while the toad inflates its body to try and make itself look too big to eat.

SMALL BUT DEADLY

One of the common toad's smallest predators is the toad fly, which lays its eggs on the toad's skin. When the eggs hatch, the maggots crawl up into the toad's nostrils, causing breathing problems. Once inside, the maggots start to eat the flesh so that eventually, the toad is completely devoured and all that is left is the bones and the skin.

The most dangerous time for toads is in the breeding season, when they gather together in large numbers and attract the attention of predators. If threatened by a predator, a toad takes a special defence posture. It stretches out its legs, gulps air into its lungs and leans its head downwards, which puffs up its body and makes it look too large for the attacker to eat.

In extreme danger, toads give off another type of poison, from two glands on their head. This white and creamy substance can paralyse an attacker and is strong enough to kill a small dog.

▼ A toad makes itself look bigger in front of an attacking grass snake. It is stretching out its legs before inflating its body.

People and toads

People can be a great threat to toads. Many of their natural habitats, including wetlands and ponds, have been destroyed or damaged over the last 50 years by new building developments. This has led toads to move into urban habitats. Here, the adults can survive well because of the availability of extra food, shelter and fewer predators.

However, while toads can benefit from urban life, they also face many dangers, particularly in gardens. Lawn mowers and strimmers maim and kill toads hiding in long grass, and garden chemicals and pest controls kill their insect prey. Toads are sometimes burned accidentally when they hide or hibernate in a bonfire. And although toads have access to garden ponds, many ponds are too small for spawning, or are difficult to get in and out of.

▲ The fragile balance of a pond or stream, which toads depend on, can easily be destroyed when rubbish is dumped there.

▼ A slow-moving toad has little chance against a motorcar.

Another human threat is from road traffic. Roads can be death traps for the slow-moving toad and most road deaths take place during the toads' annual journey to their breeding ponds. In some places, where toads are known to cross certain roads every year, local people protect them by collecting them in buckets and gently tipping them out on the other side of the road. Tunnels are also built beneath roads for toads to cross safely (see box on page 15).

Toad Life Cycle

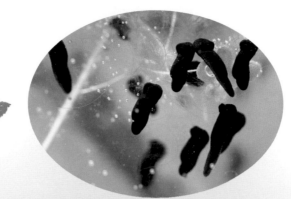

1 Toad eggs are laid in March, in pondweed or other vegetation. After 10 days, the tadpoles hatch.

2 They start to swim after two to three days and grow hind legs at 7–9 weeks old.

5 When females are 3–4 years old and males are 4–5 years old they are ready to mate.

3 The front legs grow at 11–12 weeks old.

4 At 13–14 weeks old the tail is absorbed into the body and the tiny toadlets leave the pond to live on land.

Toad Clues

Look out for the following clues to help you find signs of a toad:

Signs

Look out for road signs warning drivers about toads on the road. They are only put up where large numbers of toads usually cross the road.

Rainy days

Toads are mainly nocturnal, but they often come out to hunt on dull or rainy days, when they don't need to avoid the hot, drying effects of sunshine.

Toad spawn

Look for toad spawn in ponds during the spring. You can tell the difference between toad and frog spawn because toad spawn is arranged in strands whereas frog spawn is laid in clumps.

Croaking

Listen for the croaking of male toads in ponds, on early evenings in March or April. The most common toad sounds to hear are not the mating calls but the male 'release' call, when one male mistakes another for a female. This is a high-pitched 'qwark, qwark, qwark' sound.

Migration

Large numbers of toads may be seen in the spring, on their journey back to their breeding ponds.

Tadpoles

Toad tadpoles can be seen in the spring and summer months. The tadpoles are a blackish colour, darker than frog tadpoles. When they are very small, toad tadpoles may swim as a shoal.

Warning

If you see a toad, don't pick it up. The poison from its skin could irritate your skin. If you do touch a toad, you should wash your hands immediately afterwards and do not touch your mouth.

Glossary

amphibians A group of animals such as toads, frogs and newts that usually live on land but return to water to lay their eggs.

camouflage The colour or pattern of some animals that helps them to blend in with their surroundings and makes them hard to see.

carnivore An animal that eats mainly other animals.

courtship Animal behaviour that is used to attract a mate, such as a dance or call.

fertilized When the male provides sperm for the females eggs during mating so that the eggs will develop.

gills Structures on the head that allow tadpoles and fish to breathe by taking oxygen directly out of the water.

glands Organs in the body that produce chemical substances. Poison glands produce poison.

habitat The area where an animal or plant naturally lives.

hibernation When an animal passes the winter asleep, usually in a hole or den. Some toads, bats and snakes hibernate.

leaf litter The dead leaves that collect underneath trees or hedgerows.

migration When animals travel from one place to another.

nocturnal An animal that is active at night, such as a toad, hedgehog or owl.

nuptial pads The swellings that are found on three of the male toad's front toes, which grow bigger in the breeding season and help it to grip on to a female toad during mating.

omnivore An animal that eats both plants and other animals.

predator An animal that eats other animals.

prey Animals that are killed and eaten by predators.

shoal A group of tadpoles swimming together. A group of swimming fish is also called a shoal.

spawn A jelly-like mass of eggs produced by amphibians or fish.

tadpoles Young amphibians before they have grown legs.

toadlets Young toads that have just developed out of the tadpole stage.

vegetation Plant life that provides shelter or food for animals.

wetlands A marshy area of land.

Finding Out More

Other books to read

Animal Classification by Polly Goodman (Hodder Wayland, 2004)

Animal Young: Amphibians by Rod Theodorou (Heinemann, 1999)

Circle of Life: Pond Life by David Stewart (Watts, 2002)

Classifying Living Things: Classifying Amphibians by Andrew Solway (Heinemann, 2003)

Food Chains and Webs: River Food Chains by Emma Lynch (Heinemann, 2004)

From Egg to Adult: The Life Cycle of Amphibians by R. & L. Spilsbury (Heinemann, 2004)

How Things Grow: From Tadpole to Frog by Sally Morgan (Chrysalis, 2003)

Life Cycles: Frogs and other Amphibians by Sally Morgan (Chrysalis, 2001)

Life Cycles: From Tadpole to Frog by Gerard Legg and David Stewart (Watts, 1998)

Living Nature: Amphibian by Angela Royston (Chrysalis, 2002)

Microhabitats: Life in a Pond by Clare Oliver (Evans, 2002)

What's the Difference?: Amphibians by Stephen Savage (Hodder Wayland, 2002)

Wild Britain: Ponds by R. & L. Spilsbury (Heinemann, 2003)

Wild Habitats of the British Isles: Rivers and Waterways by R. & L. Spilsbury (Heinemann, 2005)

Organisations to contact

Countryside Foundation for Education
PO Box 8, Hebden Bridge HX7 5YJ
www.countrysidefoundation.org.uk
An organisation that produces training and teaching materials to help the understanding of the countryside and its problems.

English Nature
Northminster House, Peterborough, Cambridgeshire PE1 1UA
www.englishnature.org.uk
A government body that promotes the conservation of English wildlife and the natural environment.

RSPB
The Lodge, Sandy, Bedfordshire SG19 2DL
www.rspb.org.uk
A wild birds conservation charity with wildlife reserves and a website that includes an A-Z of UK birds, news, surveys and webcams about issues concerning wild birds.

Wildlife Watch
National Office, The Kiln, Waterside, Mather Road, Newark, Nottinghamshire NG24 1WT
www.wildlifetrusts.org
The junior branch of the Wildlife Trusts, a network of local Wildlife Trusts caring for nearly 2,500 nature reserves, from rugged coastline to urban wildlife havens, protecting a huge number of habitats and species.

Index

Page numbers in **bold** refer to a photograph or illustration.

amphibians 4, 6, **18**, 24

burrow 7, 13, 16

camouflage 4
croaking 22, 23, 29

defence **24**, **25**
diet **18–19**
distribution **4**

eggs **6**, **8**, 9, 23
eyesight **5**, 10, 20, 21

feet **4**, **5**
frogs 6, 7

gardens **14**, 17, 26

habitats 4, **12–15**
hatching 6, 9, **28**
hibernation 4, **16–17**

holes 4, **16**
hunting **20**, **21**

legs **4**, **5**, 7, **11**
lifespan 24

mating 5, **22**, **23**, 29
migration **29**

names 4
nocturnal 13

people 26–27
poison 4, 5, 7, 24
predators 8, 14, **18**, **24–25**
prey 5, **18–21**

roads 15, **27**, **29**

size 4, **5**
skin **4**, 7, **12**, 27
spawn **8**, **9**, **29**

species 4, 6–7
superstitions 27
swallowing **21**
swimming 9, **10**, **11**

tadpoles 4, 8, **9–11**, **18**
tail 10, **11**
teeth 7, 21
temperature 8, 10, 16, 17
toadlets 4, **11**
toads
    Couch's spadefoot 7
    firebellied **7**
    midwife **6**
tongue 5, 10, **19**, **20**
tunnels **15**, 27

walking 7, **17**
water **8–11**, 12, 19
weather 6, 8, 10, 17
weight 4